Betsy's
Blue F...

MW01108996

Meals Like Mom's . . .
Now Low-fat, Delicious, and Fast!

By Betsy Barenholtz Rudolph

Happy Cooking !! :)

Betsy Barenholtz Rudolph

July 2003

Library of Congress Catalog Card Number: 96-92868
ISBN 0-9655228-0-6

Betsy Barenholtz Rudolph, Author
Kimberly S. Fish, Editor

Published by BBR Publishing
P.O. Box 280
Jerseyville, Illinois 62052

To order copies of
Betsy's Blue Plate Specials
send check for $15.95 plus $2.50 for shipping and handling.
Illinois residents add $1.15 sales tax per book.

Send to:
Betsy Rudolph
P.O. Box 280
Jerseyville, Illinois 62052

Acknowledgements ✎

My sincere thank you to my husband, **David Rudolph**, for his continuous support through his endurance in taste testing and creative mind in both success and failures. He has truly inspired me to reach new goals in my professional and personal life. Thanks to my daughter, **Alexandra**, and my son, **Andrew**, for their humor, excitement, love, and of course, the one-bite taste testing. Special thanks to **Dorothy Powers**, who takes care of us all.

Thank you to my best friend and editor, **Kimberly Fish**, and her husband, **Wayne**, for belief and commitment in this book to help make it happen.

A big FAT thank you to . . .

My Family:
Papa, **William Lee**, who has filled some big shoes in my life.
Parents, **Barbara & Milton Hieken**, for honest opinions I always need.
David's parents, **Jean & Harvey Rudolph**, for helping out all the time.
Bob & Judy Barenholtz for their printing and publishing advice.
Bill & Suzi Barenholtz for their great food ideas.
Barbie & Ron Present for encouraging phone calls.
Steve Rudolph & Anna Voytovich for professional advice.

My Friends and Acquaintances:
Diane Alexander for referring me to the printing company.
Susan Allen who helped keep everything in perspective.
Joe Ancona for his book advice.
Ginny Brooks for her countless books on loan.
Sarah Brockman for helping me fix the unfixables
Carol Cookson in Dr. Mallin's office for many helpful suggestions.
Bob Cyphers who steered me in the right direction.
Jane Dougherty for her help on the cover design.
Dawn Dwyer for morning walks and talks.
Nancy Enloe for marketing ideas.
Heidi Fendelman for books used in research
Jane Goldberg for the big picture discussion.
Terry Hieken who gave cookbook advice.
Maggie Holmes for babysitting while I created.
Sharon Hudalla who assisted in preparation for my first class.
Maxine Korte for giving me a reference.
Sue Landon for the many magazines and publicity advice
Lydia Martin for advice and newspaper article.
Nancy McCabe for Project Shape-up and encouragement.
Patty Padawer for giving me the chance to gain credibility.
Donna Petro who had confidence in my teaching ability.
Karen Williams for her encouragement.
Sinclair Foods for letting me browse the store in search of nutritional info.

Table of Contents _____ ❧

A Note From Betsy _____

The first part of this book offers many suggestions to making your meals healthier and the preparation easier. It explains many ways to enjoy your favorite foods without losing all the flavors and textures. Read it as though it were a textbook and highlight the points of special interest to you. Add your own notes in the spaces provided to make this your personalized book. Have fun experimenting with your family to find what works for you.

Part two is the cookbook portion, and it unveils the daily meals consisting of the comfort foods you love to eat--but now modified to stay within your daily fat gram requirements. The menu ideas and recipes are a guide for a full week of cooking, but mix and match days or even meals according to your preferences and needs. I hope you enjoy some of my personal notes or thoughts which I couldn't resist adding a time or two.

Celebrate this first step to healthier meals. It's tough to get started, but congratulations on making the effort in using this book. You're on your way! In the fast-paced world in which we live, we are always on the go, yet somehow, our lives are more sedentary than previous generations. By becoming more physically active and watching our fat intake, we can live better and feel better about ourselves.

Enjoy this book packed with easy-to-read important information that I know will be helpful to you. It's been my pleasure to share it with you.

Betsy

* Fat has no taste, but it enhances the food's flavor and texture. Sometimes when we are cooking low-fat foods, we miss the full flavor from fat that we enjoy. This book will help you learn how to cook low-fat without giving up any of the taste.

* Don't be intimidated with number of ingredients.

* Start out with the right ingredients. Keep staples on hand.

* Measure out all ingredients before starting just like they do on TV.

* Trim all visible fat from meat. Remove poultry skin.

* Substitute low-fat or fat-free products. If this does not appeal to you, use half of the amount of meat, dairy products, and/or condiments called for in the recipe.

* Choose fresh foods or frozen foods instead of the processed foods. Processed foods have a lot of hidden calories, fat, and sodium.

* Do not season foods with salt. Try using salt-free substitutions or lemon wedges.

* Convenience foods can also save time and waste. Bag salads and vegetables, dried or frozen onions, chopped garlic can save time.

* Double favorite recipes and freeze for later use, or you can freeze half of a recipe if it's too big for your family's appetites.

* Fix dinner when it is a good time for you. Reheat in microwave when you are ready to eat. Best time for me to prepare food is when kids are napping.

* Invite a friend (or friends) over for dinner. Start a low-fat dinner club.

Fatty Fat Facts _____

* Animal fat is a saturated fat.

* Saturated fat is found in meat, poultry skin, milk, cream, butter, and cheese.

* Vegetable fat is a polyunsaturated fat.

* Polyunsaturated fat is found in corn oil, margarine, mayonnaise, and salad dressing.

* Monounsaturated fat is the safest fat.

* Monounsaturated fat is found in olive oil, avocados and nuts.

Did you know ???

1 gram of fat = 9 calories
1 gram of protein or carbohydrate = 4 calories
14 grams of vegetable fat (1 tablespoon) = 125 calories

Measuring Down _____ ❦

* It's easy to start taking the fat out bit by bit without much taste difference if you start out a little at a time. Your family will not notice if done gradually.

* Simply subtract a measured amount of fat from your favorite recipe increasing the measurement taken out each time until your family complains.

Big mistake: Telling them beforehand that you've altered the recipe.

dash	=	less than 1/8 teaspoon
3 teaspoons	=	1 Tablespoon
4 Tablespoons	=	1/4 cup
5 1/3 Tablespoons	=	1/3 cup
8 Tablespoons	=	1/2 cup

Personal Notes _____ ❦

_____
_____
_____
_____
_____
_____
_____
_____
_____

Steaming Vegetables

* Steaming vegetables is an excellent way to serve fresh or frozen vegetables. It seals in a fresh flavor and vitamins are not cooked out of the vegetables.

* Vegetables may be steamed in a bamboo steamer or a collapsible basket.

* Fresh or frozen carrots, green beans, cauliflower, and broccoli take 8 to 10 minutes to steam.

* Zucchini, squash, and other soft vegetables take 5 to 7 minutes to steam.

* Place one inch of water in sauce pan or skillet. Heat until boiling. Place vegetables in steamer. Cover. Reduce heat and steam until tender.

* Lemon, spices, and other fresh herbs may be added to water for additional taste, if desired.

Tasty Vegetable Tips

* Replace salt with a squeeze from a fresh lemon slice after vegetables are cooked.

* Minced red or yellow pepper adds color and texture.

* Dash of reduced sodium soy sauce gives extra zip to vegetables. (Or add equal parts regular soy sauce and water for a better flavor.)

* Baked/roasted garlic mixed in cooked vegetables brings out a sweet and nutty flavor.

* Salads are one of America's favorite foods. The salad dressing is usually loaded with fat and calories. Get the fat out as you experience a low-fat salad crunch.

* Replace oil in vinaigrette-type dressings by reducing the oil to 1 teaspoon per serving and replace the remaining amount of oil with water, low-fat, low-sodium chicken broth, fruit juice, or fruit nectar.

* When using a reduced oil vinaigrette or creamy dressing, use the oil mister idea (See Oil Mister) to help the dressing stick to the salad and be evenly distributed for a satisfying taste.

* Use a full-flavor vinegar, such as balsamic or one that is already flavored, for a fun start to your salad.

* In creamy dressings, replace fat with low-fat buttermilk or fat-free yogurt--plain or lemon flavored.

* If these steps for reducing fat are too severe for your palate, start out by taking one tablespoon of oil or fat out at a time until you are accustomed to the new flavor. (See Measuring Down)

* *A way to enjoy the essence of oil with less fat.*

* Oil Mister steps:

    1. Pour olive or canola oil into a clean plant mister.
    2. Mist the salad with oil--one squirt per serving.
    3. Add 1 Tablespoon any type reduced fat dressing to the salad mixture. Toss.
    4. Mist the salad again--one squirt per serving.
    5. Add another Tablespoon of dressing. Toss.
    6. Let the salad rest 10 minutes for flavors to blend.

* *This sounds like a lot of trouble (Editor's note), but it's really a simple way to reduce your fat intake without sacrificing flavor. (Author's rebuttal)*

* Other uses for the oil mister:

    1. Mist olive oil on steamed veggies for a European flavor.
    2. Mist olive oil on bread instead of buttering.
    3. Mist canola oil on popcorn not made with oil so salt substitute or other flavor-enhancing spices will adhere.
    4. Non-fat cooking sprays may be replaced with oil mister adding only a minimum of fat.

* One squirt of oil equals 1/2 gram of fat or less.

    Yes, I did painstakingly measure this.

Menu Planning Tips _____

* Make sure you are satisfied with your meal selections. *Satisfaction is the key.*

* It's okay to personalize your menu by exchanging favorite foods within the same food groups that have the similar nutritional values.

* You may also want to switch the order of your main meal depending on your lifestyle and personal needs.

* Nutritional content of your meals within the daily menu may be shifted as long as you balance the rest of your meals.

Breakfast is a great time to . . .

* Be a Jack Sprat and eat no fat.

* Enhance toast with the flavor of apple butter, jelly, or all-fruit spread instead of margarine.

* Take the fat out of your coffee by using skim milk or nonfat creamer for coffee.

* Start your daily requirement of calcium by drinking milk or eating yogurt.

* Save on daily protein or no-fat protein portions to reserve for lunch or dinner.

Morning snack is a great time to . . .

* Eat fruit and/or carbohydrates to help curb your appetite until your next meal.

Lunch is a great time to . . .

* Eat just 2 ounces of protein (beans, fish, chicken, or turkey) surrounded by lots of veggies and complex carbohydrates (bread, cereal, rice, or pasta) to fill you up with taste and vitamins.

Afternoon snack is a great time to . . .

* Give yourself a break and enjoy a piece of fruit, a carbohydrate, and/or a calcium treat for an afternoon delight.

Dinner is a great time to . . .

* Relax to the sights, sounds, and smells of a home-cooked meal.

* Eat from all the food groups within your food plan for the day.

* Celebrate your healthful menu plan by saving your sweet treat for an evening snack.

As long as it's before exercising and not too late.

Breakfast Ideas

* Oversleep and in a hurry?

* Grab a piece of fruit, a cup of milk, and a muffin. Out the door!

* Grab a bagel. Add 1 Tablespoon light cream cheese (flavor of your choice) and fresh fruit. On your way!

* Grab the low-fat cottage cheese and fruit or a low-fat fruited yogurt. A quick fix!

Lunch and Dinner Ideas

* No time? Do a big salad with sliced turkey and fat-free dressing on the side. Serve with roll.

* Don't want to cook? Place low-fat or fat-free luncheon meats on two pieces of bread. Serve with veggies and low-fat dip.

* On the run? Try cottage cheese, sliced tomatoes, and crackers. There's a chance you'll like it.

* At least once a week, serve a "MustgoMeal." Everything left in the refrigerator *must go*!
  Try to stick to your food allowances.

Snack Ideas

* Choose low-fat snacks: pretzels, popcorn, fruit, fresh veggies and dip, frozen yogurt, ice cream, flavored rice cakes, corn cakes, graham crackers, fig bars, crackers, diet soda ice cream float.

Shopping Guidelines

* Grocery shopping can be a chore. Plan what you are to buy before going to the store. Use the grocery list in the back of the book as a shopping guide for your *Blue Plate Specials*.

* *Plan*
* Have a working/running grocery list going at all times. Keep it in a convenient location in your kitchen. Have other family members add to the list as items become low rather than waiting until it runs out so you have to raid the neighbor's pantry.

* *Never Go Hungry*
* Do all grocery shopping after eating a meal or a healthy and fulfilling snack. Wait until you are home before eating anything purchased from the store. This includes the candy bar you threw in the grocery cart.

* *Read Labels*
* Read labels and decide which product is the best for your own situation. Low-fat and/or fat-free are not always the best choice. Watch out for sodium and sugar. Fat-free has less than 1/2 gram fat per serving. Low-fat has 3 grams of fat or less per serving. Low calorie has 40 calories per serving or less.

* *Stay On The Outside Aisles*
* The outside aisles usually have the produce, meats, dairy, and grain sections. The inside aisles have the cookies, chips, baking products. Don't buy it if you aren't supposed to eat it. Stick to your grocery list and you will be less tempted.

* Use salad plates instead of dinner plates. The plate looks full, and less will look like more.

* Serve food away from dinner table. Do not have serving bowls on the table.

* Eat slowly. It takes 20 minutes for the stomach to tell the brain it is full. Maybe less if you have an exceptional brain

    (1)   Put down fork and put hands in lap between each bite.
    (2)   Take next bite only after food from previous mouthful has been chewed and swallowed.
    (3)   Have a drink of water between bites.
    (4)   Wait 30 seconds between bites of food.

* If eating out in a restaurant and the low-fat, fat-free salad dressings are not to your liking, order the regular salad dressing served on the side. Use less dressing by dipping fork into salad dressing and then take your usual bite of lettuce.

* Eat portions according to your personal eating plan. Measure, if necessary.

* It is okay to have second helpings, but wait five minutes before serving it to see if you really want it. Serve only half the amount on the second portion. Then if still hungry, eat the other half of the halved serving. You have now had three helpings but only two servings. If still not satisfied, rather than having another portion, eat a vegetable or fruit.

* There are no foods off limits. Plan for them. Figure out how you can make them lower in fat without sacrificing flavor and texture.

* Let the kids eat fast foods once in a while. Serve healthful foods at home.

* It is important to feel satisfied. Make your menu planning work for you.

Personal Notes _____

_____

_____

_____

_____

_____

_____

_____

_____

_____

_____

_____

* Focus on the positive--what you are doing for yourself, not what you are *not* doing.

* Educate yourself with food information whenever possible. Read magazines, books, etc.

* Learn new ways to prepare your favorite foods; for example, oven-baked fried chicken instead of skillet fried chicken.

* Give up one thing at a time. Take the cheese off of the hamburger. Switch to low-fat milk from whole milk, eventually enjoying skim milk.

* Be open-minded and creative.

* Plan dinner around vegetables and grains--not around the meat.

* Use half the amount of meats substituting 8 ounces of sliced mushrooms and 1 chopped onion for every half pound of hamburger omitted.

* To reduce fat in hamburger, change from ground beef to extra lean ground chuck and then to ground round.

* When cooking a casserole or soups with hamburger meat, rinse hamburger meat after cooking with hot water. Clean off skillet and place drained meat back into skillet.

* Before cooking any type of meat, trim off all visible fat. This will reduce fat content by 9 percent.

* Marinate less tender cuts of beef 4-12 hours for best results.

* Marinade Ideas:
  Nonfat bottled Italian salad dressing.
  Mix equal amounts of Teriyaki sauce and water.

* Choose a London broil or a round steak for approximately 4 grams of fat per 3-ounce serving.

* Sirloin steak and kabobs equal approximately 6 grams of fat.

* Filet mignon and strip steak have approximately 8-9 grams of fat.

* If grilling outside, place the trimmed fat around the meat to achieve the smoky flavor you are anticipating.

* Use half the amount of dairy products, sugars, or oils in a recipe.

* Add more of the grains, vegetables, or fruits in a recipe when taking out the fat.

* Use half of the regular product and half of the low-fat, fat-free similar product to equal the recipe amount.

* Reduce fat and sugar by half the amount the recipe calls for without a noticeable difference.

Favorite Fat Substitutes _____

Fatty Faux Pas	Satisfying Subs
Butter/Margarine	Non-aerosol butter spray Liquid butter substitute Low-fat, low-sodium chicken broth Non-stick cooking spray
Oil	Olive or canola Low-fat, low-sodium chicken broth Non-stick cooking spray Oil mister
Cream/Milk	Nonfat evaporated skim milk Plain nonfat yogurt Skim milk
Mayonnaise	Low-fat or fat-free mayonnaise Nonfat yogurt, drained Low-fat or fat-free sour cream Any combination of the above with a dash of dijon mustard

Eggs	Egg substitute, follow directions
	2 eggs equals 1 egg plus 2 egg whites
	
	2 egg recipe: 5 egg whites
	                    pinch of baking soda
	                    pinch of baking powder
	                    yellow food coloring

Fatty Faux Pas	Satisfying Subs
Chips	Low-fat baked potato chips Low-fat baked tortilla chips Low-fat popcorn Pretzels

(In Baking)

Fatty Faux Pas	Satisfying Subs
Oil	Replace oil with applesauce to equal the amount of oil omitted. For desired consistency, replace oil with equal amounts of applesauce and non-fat yogurt equal to amount of oil omitted. Replace the oil in a fruited recipe by increasing that fruit to equal the amount of oil omitted.
Pie Crust	Phyllo dough Low-fat crushed graham crackers
Butter in Frosting	Marshmallow cream
Chocolate	Cocoa powder 1 ounce chocolate = 3 Tablespoons powder

Low-Fat Cooking Staples _____

These are some of the basic low-fat items to have on hand at all times making low-fat cooking easier for you.

applesauce
beans
butter substitute
canned light fruits
canned low-sodium tomatoes
canned tuna in water
canola oil
couscous
dried bread crumbs
dijon mustard
fat-free Parmesan
herbs and spices of your personal preference
low-fat, low-sodium chicken broth
low-fat or fat-free mayonnaise
low-fat or fat-free sour cream
low-fat or fat-free yogurt
nonfat evaporated skim milk
nonfat Italian dressing
nonfat non-stick cooking spray
oatmeal
olive oil
pasta
rice
salsa
skim milk
soy sauce
tomato paste
vinegars (flavored)

Helpful Utensils in the Low-fat Kitchen
bamboo steamer or vegetable steamer
kitchen scissors
3 misters for olive oil, canola oil, and water
non-stick skillet

Daily Meal Plan #1

Breakfast
Waffles
Strawberries
Syrup
Milk

350 Calories
0 grams Fat
515 mg. Sodium

Lunch
Cheesy Quesadilla
Very Veggie Chili
Pineapple Slices

355 Calories
8 grams Fat
770 mg. Sodium

Dinner
Roast Beef Dinner
Steamed Green Beans
Dreamy Mashed Potatoes
Applesauce

325 Calories
4 grams Fat
275 mg. Sodium

❦ Waffles

Preparation Time: About 5 minutes
Cooking Time: About 5 minutes

Dry Ingredients
1 1/4 cup all purpose flour
1 Tablespoon sugar
2 teaspoon baking powder
1/2 teaspoon baking soda

Liquid Ingredients
1/4 cup egg substitute equal to 1 egg
1 cup non fat vanilla yogurt
2 Tablespoons applesauce

Non-stick cooking spray

1. Combine dry ingredients in large bowl.
2. Mix liquid ingredients in a medium bowl.
   Add to dry ingredients until just moistened.
3. Prepare waffle iron with non-stick cooking spray. Preheat and pour 1/2 of mixture on griddle.
4. Cook until light comes on. May need to toast in toaster oven for a crispier texture.

Yield: *8 servings (4-inch waffle per serving)*
1 serving contains: 120 Calories   0 g. Fat   225 mg. Sodium

❦ Strawberries

Heat strawberries with maple syrup for a sweet addition to your waffles. Serve a cold glass of milk with breakfast.

❦ Cheesy Quesadillas

Preparation Time: About 1 minute
Cooking Time: About 3 minutes

1 flour tortilla per serving
1 slice (3/4-ounce) processed cheese of your choice

*Nonfat cheese will reduce fat grams and calories.

1   Preheat non-stick skillet to medium hot temperature.
2.   Place tortilla on prepared skillet. Turn tortilla over after 30 seconds to warm both sides.
3.   Place cheese on the inside 1/2 of the tortilla. Fold in half, covering the cheese with the tortilla.
4.   Turn tortilla shell over until cheese is melted.
5.   Cut into strips and serve with salsa.

Yield: *1 serving (1 quesadilla)*
1 serving contains: 170 Calories   6.5 g. Fat   400 mg. Sodium

Note: May use microwave to heat tortilla, but it will become soggy. I prefer crisp quesadillas made in the skillet.

Lunch Alternative To Quesadilla _____ ❦

* Fix a grilled cheese by preparing a non-stick skillet with non-stick cooking spray. Place cheese between two slices of bread. Spray butter substitute on outer sides of bread. Grill on each side.

❦ Pineapple

Serve pineapple slices with quesadillas and veggie chili to become a family luncheon favorite.

❦ Very Veggie Chili

Preparation Time: About 10 minutes
Cooking Time: About 30 minutes

2 Tablespoons low-fat, low-sodium chicken broth
1 clove garlic, minced
1 large onion, chopped
1 green pepper, chopped

1 cup water

1 Tablespoon chili powder
1 Tablespoon sugar
1/2 Tablespoon cumin
1/2 Tablespoon oregano
3/4 teaspoon curry

1 can (14 1/2-ounce) low-sodium tomatoes
1 can (16-ounce) dark red kidney beans, drained
1 can (15-ounce) garbanzo beans, drained

1. Saute onion, garlic, peppers in broth until soft over a medium low heat.
2. Add water and heat to temperature of onion mixture. Continue to add the rest of the ingredients. Bring to a boil. Reduce heat, cover. Simmer 15 to 30 minutes until ready to serve.

Yield: *6 servings (1 cup per serving)*
1 serving contains: 150 Calories   1.5 g. Fat   445 mg. Sodium

Veggie Chili Hints

* May reduce sodium up to 30 percent by heating beans in a saucepan for 3 minutes on medium heat and rinsing under warm water. Drain thoroughly.

* May want to use low-sodium beans.

* This may be made early in the day and placed in the crock-pot. Cook on low heat up to 8 hours or high heat 4 hours or less. This is also great the next day when the flavors have had a chance to blend.

* Pour unused chicken broth into ice cube trays to freeze for later use.

Personal Notes

_____

_____

_____

_____

_____

_____

_____

_____

❦ All-Day Roast Beef

Preparation Time: About 5 minutes
Cooking Time: 6 to 8 hours, unattended

1 (2-pound) eye of the round, trimmed of fat
1/3 cup chili sauce
1/4 cup dried chopped onion

1. Place beef in crock-pot.
2. Pour in chili sauce and add onion.
3. Cook on low heat 6 to 8 hours or high heat 4 to 6 hours.
4. Remove roast from crock-pot and let rest 20 minutes before slicing. Keep juice warm in crock-pot until ready to serve.

Yield: *8 servings (3 ounces per serving)*
1 serving contains: 155 Calories   4 g. Fat   200 mg. Sodium

Leftover Roast Beef Idea _____ ❦

* For a beefy taco salad, line salad bowl with one serving of low-fat tortilla chips. Add salad options of your choice. Shred 2 ounces of leftover roast beef. Dress with a fat-free ranch or French salad dressing, salsa, and a dollop of low-fat sour cream for fun.

❦ Steamed Green Beans

Serve steamed green beans with a squeeze from a fresh lemon for extra zip.

🍂 Dreamy Mashed Potatoes

Preparation Time: About than 5 minutes
Cooking Time: Less than 25 minutes

4 medium potatoes, peeled or unpeeled
2 cups low-fat, low-sodium chicken broth
1/2 cup nonfat evaporated skim milk

1. Boil cut-up potatoes in chicken broth until tender. Drain and reserve liquid.
2. When mashing potatoes, use nonfat evaporated skim milk in place of milk.
3. Omit margarine and butter. May use butter substitute.

Yield: *2/3 cup equals one serving*
1 serving contains: 100 Calories   0 g. Fat   75 mg. Sodium

Mashed Tater Tips_____

   * Prepare instant potatoes substituting low-fat, low-sodium chicken broth for the water called for from the box. Use non-fat evaporated skim milk in place of milk or cream. Omit all margarine or butter. May use butter substitute, if desired.

   * For a gravy topper, use the au jus from crock-pot or add corn starch to thicken.

🍂 Applesauce

Jazz up prepared applesauce with cinnamon to complete this meal. Serve it warm for an added surprise.

Daily Meal Plan #2

Breakfast
French Toast
Hot Apple Slices
Turkey Bacon
Milk

*270 Calories
1 grams Fat
590 mg. Sodium*

Lunch
Barbeque Beef Sandwich
Small Garden Salad
Fresh Pear

*465 Calories
6 grams Fat
930 mg. Sodium*

Dinner
Mm Mm Spaghetti Dinner
Caesar Salad
Garlic Sourdough Bread

*400 Calories
1 gram Fat
315 mg. Sodium*

❦ French Toast

Preparation Time: About 5 minutes
Cooking Time : About 12 minutes

1/4 cup egg substitute equal to 1 egg
    (per 2 slices of bread)
1 teaspoon skim milk
1/4 teaspoon vanilla extract
1/4 teaspoon cinnamon

2 slices bread of your choice

Non-stick cooking spray

1. Whisk egg, milk, vanilla, and cinnamon in a shallow bowl.
2. Prepare non-stick skillet with spray. Heat on medium low heat.
3. Dip bread into egg mixture, allowing mixture to soak in. Turn to coat both sides.
4. Place dipped bread in prepared skillet. Cook until both sides are golden brown.
5. Top with cooked apple slices. May sprinkle powdered sugar. Watch out for extra calories.

Yield: *1 serving (2 slices of toast per serving)*
1 serving contains: 120 Calories   0 g. Fat   350 mg. Sodium

French Toast Hint _____ ❦

Warm oven to 200 degrees. Place French toast in oven to keep warm while preparing enough for the whole family.

❦ Hot Apple Slices

Preparation Time: About 5 minutes
Cooking Time: About 10 minutes

1 apple, sliced thinly
1/4 cup orange juice
1/4 teaspoon vanilla extract
1 Tablespoon brown sugar
1/8 teaspoon nutmeg
1/8 teaspoon cinnamon

1. Combine all ingredients into a small saucepan. Bring to a boil.
2. Cover and simmer about 5 minutes until apples are soft.
3. Place over French toast.

Yield: *4 servings (1/4 apple per serving)*
1 serving contains: 30 Calories   0 mg. Fat   0 mg. Sodium

❦ Turkey Bacon

Add some turkey bacon to this hearty French toast breakfast, and enjoy a cold glass of milk.

Bits on Bacon _____

* To save time later, cook entire package of bacon and then refrigerate in an airtight container. Reheat for other breakfast and lunch needs.

* Substitute Canadian bacon for a different taste while still saving fat grams.

🍄 Barbecue Beef Sandwich

Preparation Time: About 2 minutes
Cooking Time: About 5 minutes

1/2 cup leftover au jus
12 ounces leftover roast beef, cut up
1/2 cup barbecue sauce
4 hamburger buns, toasted if desired

1.   Heat roast beef and juice in a small saucepan until liquid is absorbed, stirring occasionally.
2.   Add barbecue sauce. Heat thoroughly.
3.   Serve on hamburger buns.

Yield: *4 servings (3-ounce sandwiches)*
1 serving contains: 335 Calories   6.0 g. Fat   640 mg. Sodium

🍄 Small Garden Salad

Salad Options
lettuce of your choice and vegetables

Dressing
2 Tablespoons fat-free salad dressing of your choice

1. Mix salad ingredients together. Use oil mister and toss.

Yield: *4 servings (1 1/2 cup per serving)*
1 serving contains: 50 Calories   0 g. Fat   290 mg. Sodium

🍄 Pears

Fresh pears make a light and tasty addition to this lunch.

🐌 Mm Mm Spaghetti Dinner

Preparation Time: About 5 minutes
Cooking Time: 20 minutes and crock-pot, if desired

2 Tablespoons low-sodium, low-fat chicken broth
8 mushrooms, sliced
1 large onion, chopped
2 garlic cloves, minced

1 can (10 3/4-ounce) low-sodium, low-fat tomato soup
1 can (6-ounce) tomato paste
1 bay leaf
1/2 teaspoon basil
1/2 teaspoon oregano
1/8 teaspoon thyme
2 teaspoons Worcestershire sauce
2 teaspoons sugar or substitute
1 box (16-ounce) spaghetti noodles

1. In medium pan, saute onion, mushroom, and garlic in chicken broth until soft.
2. Combine remaining seasonings. Bring to boil. Reduce heat and simmer until ready to serve.
3. While sauce is simmering, prepare pasta noodles according to package, if serving immediately.

Yield: *6 servings (1/2 cup Sauce, 1 cup Pasta per serving)*
1 serving contains: 275 Calories   1 g. Fat   180 mg. Sodium

Note: Pour sauce in crock-pot and cook on low up to 3 hours, if desired.

Before serving, take bay leaf out. A child once asked if a window was left open and leaves blew in on our dinner.

❦ Caesar Salad

Preparation Time: About 10 minutes
Chilling Time: Best when prepared 8 to 12 hours in advance letting flavors blend. May keep in refrigerator up to 1 week.

Salad Options
lettuce of your choice
tomatoes
onion
mushrooms
fat-free croutons

Dressing
1/3 cup fat-free mayonnaise
2 Tablespoons fat-free grated Parmesan cheese
1 Tablespoon freshly squeezed lemon juice
1 clove garlic, minced
1 1/2 Tablespoon anchovy paste

Dressing
1.   Combine all ingredients in blender.
2.   Blend until smooth.

Salad
1.   Place salad ingredients in bowl.
2.   Use oil mister and toss with dressing.

Yield: *6 servings (1 1/2 cups salad, 1 Tablespoon dressing per serving)*
1 serving contains: 45 Calories   0 g. Fat   100 mg. Sodium

❦ Garlic Sourdough Bread

Top bread with butter substitute, garlic powder, and paprika.
Toast in oven for a no-fat favorite.

Daily Meal Plan #3

Breakfast
Yogurt Shake-up
Granola Crunch

375 Calories
4 grams Fat
265 mg. Sodium

Lunch
Macaroni and Cheese
Mixed Veggies
Fresh Apple

390 Calories
8 grams Fat
380 mg. Sodium

Dinner
Oven Fried Chicken Breast
Rice on the Wild Side
Steamed Broccoli
Fruited Garden Salad

470 Calories
3 grams Fat
500 mg. Sodium

🍎 Yogurt Shake-up

Preparation Time: About 5 minutes

1 small banana, cut up
4 fresh or frozen strawberries
1/4 cup orange juice
1/2 cup skim milk
1/2 cup fat-free vanilla yogurt

1. Place all ingredients in a blender.
2. Blend until smooth or desired consistency.

Yield: *1 serving (12 ounces per serving)*
1 Serving contains: 175 Calories   0 g. Fat   75mg. Sodium

Personal Notes _____ 🍎

_____

_____

_____

_____

_____

_____

_____

_____

_____

🐛Granola Crunch

Preparation Time: About 10 minutes
Cooking Time : About 50 minutes

Dry Ingredients
1/4 cup quick-cooking oats
1/2 cup wheat flake cereal
2 Tablespoons chopped almonds
2 Tablespoons unsweetened shredded coconut

Coating
6 ounces of canned apple juice, thawed
2 Tablespoons brown sugar

Fruits
1/2 cup raisins
1/4 cup pitted prunes, chopped
1/4 cup dried apricots

Non-stick cooking spray

1. Preheat oven to 350. Spray baking sheet.
2. Combine dry ingredients in a large bowl. Mix well.
3. Combine juice and brown sugar in a small bowl. Add to dry mixture. Toss well to coat.
4. Spread mixture on prepared baking sheet. Mist with canola oil mister.
5. Bake 40 to 50 minutes until golden brown, stirring every 20 minutes to promote even browning.
6. Stir in fruits. Bake an additional 5 minutes. Cool.

Yield: *8 servings (1/2 cup per serving)*
1 serving contains: 200 Calories   4 g. Fat   195 mg. Sodium

Note: This will keep up to 2 weeks in air-tight container.

❦ Macaroni & Cheese

Preparation Time: About 3 minutes
Cooking Time: About 10 minutes

4 cup macaroni noodle, cooked
4 slices (3/4-ounce) processed cheese of your choice
1 Tablespoon skim milk

1. Cook pasta according to package directions. Drain well.
2. Place noodles into a small bowl, add milk and cheese to noodles.
3. Heat in microwave 30 seconds to melt cheese, if necessary. Mix well.

Yield: 4 serving (1 cup per serving)
1 serving contains: 270 Calories   7 g. Fat   310 mg. Sodium

Note: Cook extra noodles when cooking noodles for spaghetti dinner. Use leftover noodles, moistened with water and heat in microwave. Add cheese and heat in microwave for a few seconds until cheese is melted spending less time in the kitchen.

❦ Mixed Veggies

Enjoy steamed vegetables, leftover if possible, and an apple to complement this quick lunch.

🐝 Oven Fried Chicken

Preparation Time: About 15 minutes
Cooking Time: 40 minutes

6 skinless, boneless chicken breast halves
non-stick cooking spray

1/2 cup non-fat plain yogurt
1 teaspoon skim milk
dash of Tabasco hot sauce

1 cup flour
1 cup Italian bread crumbs
1 Tablespoon Old Bay Seasoning
1 Tablespoon paprika
1 teaspoon garlic powder
1/2 teaspoon Creole seasoning
1/2 teaspoon basil
1/2 teaspoon oregano

1. Preheat oven to 400. Prepare cooking sheet with spray.
2. Mix yogurt, milk and Tabasco in a shallow bowl.
3. Combine flour, bread crumbs, and seasonings in a plastic bag. Shake to mix well.
4. Dip chicken into yogurt mixture. Put in bag and shake.
5. Place well-coated chicken on prepared cookie sheet. Lightly coat chicken with non-stick spray.
6. Place cookie sheet on bottom rack. Bake 40 minutes turning chicken over after 20 minutes to brown evenly.

Yield: *6 servings (4 ounces per serving)*
1 serving contains: 225 Calories   2 g. Fat   370 mg. Sodium

Leftover Chicken Idea

Try this great lunch idea--chicken Parmesan. Heat leftover chicken with leftover spaghetti sauce. Sprinkle with fat-free parmesan cheese. Lunch is ready in seconds.

Chicken Tidbits

* For a crispier crust, lightly mist coated chicken with water instead of non-stick spray.

* When turning chicken, remove cooking sheet from oven so breading won't stick to pan, allowing steam to escape.

* Cut chicken breasts into bite size pieces following above recipe for fun chicken nuggets.

* For a change of taste, season chicken with black pepper, dip in skim milk, and roll into breading of crushed corn flakes, frosted corn flakes, or crispy rice cereal. Bake in prepared glass dish at 400 degrees for 40 minutes.

Steamed Broccoli

Steam broccoli and serve as a colorful addition to your meal.

🍒 Rice on the Wild Side

Preparation Time: About 10 minutes
Cooking Time: 25 minutes

1 cup long grain and wild rice blend
2 cups low-fat, low-sodium chicken broth

1 stalk celery, chopped
2 teaspoons dried parsley
1 teaspoon dried chopped onion
1 bay leaf
1/4 teaspoon dried oregano

1. Follow directions on rice package substituting chicken broth for required amount of water.
2. Combine celery and seasonings to broth before bringing to boil.
3. Add rice to boiling broth and follow package directions.

Yield: *4 servings (2/3 cup per serving)*
1 serving contains: 160 Calories   *0.5 g. Fat*   *100 mg. Sodium*

🐝 Fruited Garden Salad With Raspberry Vinaigrette

Preparation Time: About 5 minutes
Chilling Time: Not necessary

Salad Options
lettuce of your choice
1 can (8-ounce) drained pineapple chunks
1 cup grapes

Dressing
1/3 cup raspberry preserves
1 Tablespoon water
1 1/2 Tablespoon rice wine vinegar
1 Tablespoon apple juice
1 teaspoon course-grained mustard
pepper, to taste
freshly squeezed lemon juice, to taste

Dressing
1. Place preserves in a small bowl or jar.
2. Add water and mix well.
3. Combine vinegar, juice, mustard to raspberry mixture.
4. Season to taste with pepper and lemon juice.

Salad
1. Place salad ingredients in bowl.
2. Use oil mister and toss with dressing.

Yield: *4 servings (1 1/2 cup salad, 2 Tablespoons dressing per serving)*
1 serving contains: 60 Calories   0 g. Fat   5 mg. Sodium

Daily Meal Plan #4

Breakfast
Egg Muffin on the Go
Apple Juice

304 Calories
4 grams Fat
425 mg. Sodium

Lunch
Fried Chicken Salad
Fresh Orange Slices

290 Calories
3 grams Fat
485 mg. Sodium

Dinner
Peppy Pizza
L'Italian Salad

225 Calories
7 grams Fat
405 mg. Sodium

🦋 Egg Muffin On The Go

Preparation time: About 3 minutes
Cooking time: About 5 minutes

1/4 cup egg substitute equal to 1 egg
1 slice turkey bacon
2 Tablespoon grated low-fat cheese
1 English muffin
Non-stick cooking spray

1. Split English muffin. Sprinkle cheese on the face of the muffin. Heat to melt cheese in toaster oven.
2. Cook 1 piece of bacon until crisp.
3. Prepare nonstick skillet with cooking spray. Scramble egg in skillet until cooked.
4. Place egg and bacon on prepared cheese muffin. Add ketchup for real take-out flavor.

Yield: *1 serving (1 muffin sandwich)*
1 serving contains: 220 Calories   *4 g. Fat*   *425 mg. Sodium*

Breakfast Alternative to Egg Muffin _____ 🦋

* Wrap egg, bacon, and cheese into a warm tortilla for a breakfast burrito. May use sausage or any other combination. Add a little salsa for extra wake-up power.

🦋 Apple Juice

Add a zesty touch to your breakfast with the tart flavor of apple juice.

❦ Fried Chicken Salad

Preparation Time: About 5 minutes

1/2 leftover oven-fried chicken breast, about 2 ounces

Salad Options
lettuce of your choice
tomatoes
green onions
mushrooms
fat-free croutons
grated low-fat cheese
carrot
celery

Dressing
2 Tablespoons fat-free honey mustard salad dressing
or any low-fat dressing of your choice.

1. Combine salad ingredients of your choice into a large bowl. Add salad dressing.
2. Reheat chicken. Cut into bite-size pieces. Place on top of salad.

Yield: *1 serving (2 cups salad, 2 Tablespoons dressing per serving))*
1 serving contains: 290 Calories   3 g. Fat   485 mg. Sodium

❦ Orange Slices

Serve fresh orange slices with salad for a satisfying lunch accompaniment.

🍒 Peppy Pizza Pie

Preparation Time: About 10 minutes
Cooking Time: 10 minutes

1 (12-inch) Italian pizza shell
1/2 onion, thinly sliced
8 mushrooms, thinly sliced
1/4 cup pepperoni flavored pizza sauce
1/4 cup finely grated pizza cheese

1. Preheat oven to 450.
2. Spread pizza sauce over pizza shell. Top with cheese, onion, and mushrooms.
3. Bake in middle rack 10 minutes until cheese is melted.

Yield: *8 servings (1 serving contains 1/8 of 12-inch pizza)*
1 serving contains: 185 Calories   6 g. Fat   385 mg. Sodium

Pizzabilities

* Freshly grated cheese has more air than packaged grated cheese so less is necessary. Low-fat medium grated cheese has the same fat grams as equal amounts of finely grated regular cheese.

* Prepare pizza and then salad. Have kids help. They seem to like to eat what they have helped create fun faces with veggies.

* For individual servings, substitute tortilla shells.

* When preparing pizza, use sauce sparingly so it doesn't overpower other flavors and make crust soggy.

🍎 L'Italian Salad

Preparation Time: About 10 minutes
Chilling Time: Refrigerate up to a week

Salad Options
lettuce of your choice
onion
mushroom
tomato

Dressing
3 teaspoons basil
3 teaspoons oregano
3 teaspoons thyme
1 teaspoon parsley
1/8 teaspoon pepper
6 ounces red wine vinegar
2 Tablespoons water

Dressing
1. Mix basil, oregano, thyme, parsley, pepper, vinegar, and water in a small bowl or jar. Mix well.

Salad
1. Place salad ingredients in large bowl.
2. Use oil mister and toss with dressing.

Yield: *4 servings (1 1/2 cup salad, 1 Tablespoon dressing per serving)*
1 serving contains: 40 Calories   1 g. Fat   15 mg. Sodium

Daily Meal Plan #5

Breakfast
Oatmeal Surprise
Banana

190 Calories
1 grams Fat
0 mg. Sodium

Lunch
Turkey Club Sandwich
Carrot Sticks

320 Calories
4 grams Fat
295 mg. Sodium

Dinner
Meatloaf
Baked Potato
Fruit Salad
Green Bean Casserole

410 Calories
10 grams Fat
340 mg. Sodium

❦ Oatmeal Surprise

Preparation Time: About 5 minutes
Cooking Time : About 5 minutes

1 3/4 cup skim milk
1 teaspoon cinnamon
1/2 teaspoon apple pie spice
1/4 cup raisins

1 cup quick-cooking oatmeal
2 Tablespoons brown sugar

1. Bring milk, spices and raisins to a boil in a medium saucepan.
2. Stir in oatmeal. Cook 1 minute. Stir.
3. Remove from heat. Cover. Let stand a few minutes. Sprinkle with brown sugar.

Yield: *6 serving (2/3 cup per serving)*
1 serving contains: 110 Calories   1 g. Fat   30 mg. Sodium

❦ Banana

A banana is the ideal fruit addition for this cozy breakfast.

🍂 Turkey Club Sandwich

Preparation time: About 5 minutes

2 ounces leftover turkey breast, sliced
1 slice turkey bacon
1 thin slice cranberry sauce
lettuce
honey mustard, to taste
2 slices fat-free sourdough bread, toasted
   (or any bread of your choice)

1. Spread mustard on toasted sourdough bread slice.
2. Top with turkey, bacon, cranberry, and lettuce.

Yield: *1 Serving (1 sandwich per serving)*
1 serving contains: 280 Calories   4 g. Fat   295 mg. Sodium

🍂 Carrot Strips

Carrot strips add crunch to this sandwich that makes your taste buds dance with delight.

Personal Notes _____ 🍂

_____

_____

_____

_____

_____

🐝 Meatloaf Dinner

Preparation Time: About 5 minutes
Cooking Time: 1 hour

Loaf
1 (1 pound) extra lean ground round beef
1/4 cup dried chopped onion
1/4 cup dried parsley
1/2 cup quick-cooking oatmeal
1/4 cup egg substitute equal to 1 egg
1/2 cup skim milk
1 Tablespoon chili sauce
1/8 teaspoon pepper
1/8 teaspoon cinnamon

Sauce
1/3 cup chili sauce
1 Tablespoon brown sugar
1/2 teaspoon dry mustard

1. Preheat oven to 350. Mix all loaf ingredients into a large bowl. Place loaf into a 9 x 12 baking dish.
2. While baking for first 30 minutes, prepare the sauce.
3. Add sauce as topping and bake remaining 30 minutes.

Yield: *8 servings (4 ounces per serving)*
1 serving contains: 165 Calories   9 g. Fat   75 mg. Sodium

Leftover Meatloaf Idea_____ 🐝

Use leftover meatloaf and spaghetti sauce for pizza boats. Split small French baguettes in half. Top with leftover spaghetti sauce, bite-size meatloaf pieces, and low-fat cheese. Heat in oven until cheese is melted.

More on Meatloaf

* Meatloaf may be made early in the day or the day before. Refrigerate after step 1 until ready to bake. If there is any grease, drain before adding sauce. Don't let meatloaf fall off baking sheet. Yes, it can happen.

Baked Potato

Potato fits perfectly with this home-style meal.

❦ Fruit Salad

Fruit salad will refresh you and satisfy your sweet tooth.

Soup Suggestions

* The dry soup mixture used in the green bean casserole can be a base for low-fat cream soup. Delicious for quick lunches.

* Replace mushrooms with cooked broccoli for a cream of broccoli soup.

* Add cooked potato cubes for cream of potato soup.

❦ Green Bean Casserole

Preparation Time: About 15 minutes - 2 steps
Cooking Time: 30 minutes

Dry Soup - Step A
1 1/2 Tablespoons cornstarch
2 teaspoons low-sodium instant bouillon granules
1 teaspoon dried chopped onion
1/8 teaspoon dried basil
1/8 teaspoon dried thyme
1/8 teaspoon garlic powder
1/8 teaspoon pepper

1. Combine dry soup ingredients in a small bowl. Set aside.

Casserole Ingredients - Step B
1 Tablespoon low-fat, low-sodium chicken broth
1/2 small onion, chopped
8 mushrooms, chopped
2 cans (14 1/2-ounce) no-salt French style green beans
1 cup nonfat evaporated skim milk, cold
1/3 cup canned French style onion

1. Drain green beans and pat dry.
2. Saute onion and mushrooms in broth in small saucepan until soft over low heat. Drain. Set aside.
3. In medium saucepan over medium to low heat, combine milk to dry soup mixture. Add mushroom mixture. Stir 4 to 5 minutes until thickened. Remove from heat.
4. In 1 quart dish, combine beans with mushroom soup. Top with French onions.
5. Bake 30 minutes until bubbly.

Yield: *8 servings (1/2 cup per serving)*
1 serving contains: 105 Calories   1 g. Fat   260 mg. Sodium

Daily Meal Plan #6

Breakfast
Blueberry Muffin
Fruited Nonfat Yogurt

325 Calories
1 grams Fat
190 mg. Sodium

Lunch
Tuna Fish Sandwich
Low-Fat Chips
Fresh Peach

400 Calories
6.5 grams Fat
645 mg. Sodium

Dinner
Better Burger and Bun
Oven Fries
Chinese Slaw

355 Calories
8 grams Fat
460 mg. Sodium

🦀 Blueberry Muffin

Preparation Time: About 5 minutes
Cooking Time : About 15 to 20 minutes

Dry Ingredients
2 cups all purpose flour
1 cup quick-cooking oats
1/2 cup brown sugar
1 Tablespoon baking powder
1/2 teaspoon cinnamon
1/2 teaspoon cloves
1/4 teaspoon nutmeg

Liquid Ingredients
1 cup skim milk
1/2 cup egg substitute equal to 2 eggs
1/3 cup applesauce

Crumb topping
2 Tablespoons brown sugar
1/4 teaspoon cinnamon

1 cup fresh or frozen blueberries
Non-stick cooking spray

1. Preheat oven to 400. Prepare tin with non-stick spray.
2. Combine dry ingredients in large bowl and mix well.
3. Mix liquid ingredients. Add to dry ingredients and stir until just moistened. Gently fold in berries.
4. Pour into prepared muffin tin or use paper lined cups.
5. Combine crumb toppings in bowl. Sprinkle on muffins.
6. Bake 15 to 20 minutes until golden brown. Serve warm.

Yield: *12 servings (1 muffin per serving)*
1 serving contains: 255 Calories   1 g. Fat   15 mg. Sodium

🍒 Fruited Yogurt

Start your day with nonfat fruited yogurt as a great cool mix eaten with the homemade muffins.

Yogurt Yummies

* Add granola cereal for extra crunch.

* Top a strawberry yogurt with sliced kiwi for an exotic taste.

* A kiddie favorite is lime-flavored gelatin cubes in key lime yogurt.

* Be daring and add angel food cake cubes in any of the fruited yogurts.

❧ Tuna Fish Sandwich

Preparation Time: About 5 minutes

1 can (6-ounce) white meat tuna in spring water
1 can (8-ounce) sliced water chestnuts
2 Tablespoons chopped pecans (toasted optional)
1/4 cup fat-free or low-fat mayonnaise

4 English muffins, sliced & toasted
lettuce & tomato, optional

1. Drain tuna and chestnuts. In a medium bowl, combine tuna, chestnuts, and pecans.
2. Stir mayonnaise into tuna mixture and mix well.
3. Spread over muffin, and top with lettuce and tomato, if desired.

Yield: *4 servings (1/2 cup servings)*
1 serving contains: 210 Calories   *5 g. fat*   *495 mg. Sodium*

❧ Lowfat Potato Chips

As a side dish to the tuna sandwich, baked low-fat chips are a must. Approximately 12 chips are equal to a serving.

❧ Peach

Lunch is complete with the juicy taste of a fresh peach.

❦ Better Burger & Bun

Preparation Time: About 5 minutes
Cooking Time: 15 minutes

1 (1 pound) package ground turkey breast meat, (white meat only)
olive oil to mist on burger
4 hamburger buns, toasted

1. Heat barbeque grill to high heat. (Preheat oven to broil, if unable to cook outside)
2. Divide ground turkey into four parts for patties.
3. Squirt both sides of patty with olive oil from oil mister or apply 1/8 teaspoon of oil to burger sides.
4. Grill 7 minutes per side until juice runs clear.
5. Toast buns in toaster oven or broiler while burgers are cooking.
6. Serve with your favorite hamburger toppings. (Fat-free cheese okay, but count calories.)

Yield: *4 servings (1/4 pound per serving)*
1 serving contains: 220 Calories   3 g. Fat   300 mg. Sodium

Personal Notes ❦

_____

_____

_____

_____

_____

❦ Oven Fries

Preparation Time: About 10 minutes
Cooking Time: 40 minutes to 1 hour

4 medium potatoes
1/4 cup egg substitute equal to 1 egg
non-stick cooking spray

***Spice Options*:**
(seasonings of your choice)
Cajun seasoning
onion powder
garlic powder
pepper

1. Preheat oven to 400.
2. Spray nonstick cooking spray onto metal cookie sheet.
3. Clean and scrub potatoes leaving the skins intact.
4. Cut into 4 oval sections and then lengthwise into strips.
5. In a large bowl, combine egg substitute and spices. Add potato strips. Mix well to coat.
6. Spray nonstick cooking spray onto metal cookie sheet.
7. Place potato strips in single layer on prepared cookie sheet.
8. Bake on bottom shelf of oven until golden brown on the outside and soft on the inside. Turn every 20 minutes to promote even browning.

Yield: *4 servings (1 potato per person)*
1 serving contains: 100 Calories   *0 g. Fat*   *0 mg. Sodium*

Thoughts on Fries _____ ❦

* Kids love to eat these fries. My daughter requests these as part of her special birthday dinners.

🍒 Chinese Slaw

Preparation Time: About 10 minutes
Chilling Time: 8 to 12 hours unattended

Slaw
1 bag ready-to-use coleslaw or chopped cabbage
1 bunch green onions, sliced
1 bag low-fat beef Ramen noodles, broken
2 Tablespoons sunflower seeds, shelled

Dressing
beef seasoning packet
1/4 cup sugar
1/3 cup red wine vinegar
1/4 cup canola oil

1. Combine slaw ingredients in a large bowl.
2. Combine ingredients for dressing in a small bowl and mix well.
3. Stir dressing into slaw mixture. Mix well. Cover and refrigerate 8 to 12 hours.

Yield: *4 servings (½ cup per serving) with leftovers for the week*
1 serving contains: 105 Calories   5 g. Fat   160 mg. Sodium

Chinese Slaw Alterations_____

* To enhance flavor, toast sunflower seeds at 350 degrees for 5 minutes. Less quantity is needed.

* To reduce sodium, use half of the beef seasoning packet.

* To lower fat, omit or reduce sunflower seeds and oil.

Daily Meal Plan #7

Breakfast
Pancake Delight
Sausage
Syrup
Blueberries
Milk

400 Calories
2 grams Fat
590 mg. Sodium

Lunch
Stuffed Hot Potatoes
Fruit Salad

237Calories
1 gram Fat
300 mg. Sodium

Dinner
Turkey Breast
Sweet Potato Casserole
Parmesan Squash
Cranberry Sauce

400 Calories
2 grams Fat
160 mg. Sodium

❣ Pancake Delight

Preparation Time: About 5 minutes
Cooking Time: About 4 minutes

Dry Ingredients
3/4 cup all purpose flour
1 Tablespoon sugar
1 1/2 teaspoon baking powder
1/2 teaspoon cinnamon

Liquid Ingredients
1/4 cup egg substitute equal to 1 egg
1/4 cup skim milk
1/2 cup nonfat vanilla yogurt
1 Tablespoon applesauce

Non-stick cooking spray

1. Combine dry ingredients in large bowl. Mix well.
2. Mix liquids ingredients in a medium bowl. Add to dry ingredients until just moistened.
3. Pre-heat prepared non-stick skillet.
4. Pour 2 Tablespoons batter onto a prepared skillet. Turn pancakes over when edges are set (about 1 to 2 minutes). Flatten with spatula and cook until golden.

Yield: *6 servings (2 pancakes per serving)*
1 serving contains: 80 Calories   0 g. Fat   150 mg. Sodium

Note: May use frozen pancakes. Watch out for the fat and calories.

❦ Turkey Sausage

Preparation Time: About 10 minutes
Cooking Time: About 12 minutes

1 (one pound) ground turkey breast
1 green or red pepper finely chopped
1 cup fresh bread crumbs
    (equals 3 slices of bread finely shredded)
1/2 cup applesauce
1/2 cup egg substitute equals 2 eggs
1 Tablespoon dried chopped onion
1/4 teaspoon cayenne
1/4 teaspoon nutmeg
1/4 teaspoon allspice

Non-stick cooking spray

1. Combine food ingredients mix well.
2. Divide into 16 sections. Form each section into a patty.
3. Prepare non-stick skillet with spray and preheat to a medium heat.
4. Cook 10 to 12 minutes turning to ensure even browning.

Yield: *8 servings (2 patties per serving)*
1 serving contains: 92 Calories   2 g. Fat   150 mg. Sodium

❦ Blueberries

To get the wild blueberry flavor, mix in 1/2 cup fresh or frozen blueberries in the pancake mix. Otherwise, serve 1/2 cup blueberries per person and a nice cold glass of milk. Top pancakes with the richness of your favorite syrup.

🐛 Stuffed Hot Potato

Preparation Time: About 3 minutes
Cooking Time: 1 hour or less if using leftover potatoes

1 potato per person
1 Tablespoon skim milk, heated

Topping of your choice:
1/2 cup leftover veggie chili
1 Tablespoon low-fat shredded cheese

1. Bake potato at 400 for 1 hour or until tender. May use leftover potato and reheat.
2. Split top of potato, mix in warm milk to prevent dryness, spoon topping of your choice over potato.

Yield: *1 potato (1 potato per serving)*
1 serving contains: 177 Calories   1 g. Fat   300 mg. Sodium

Note: Go ahead and eat the skins for lots of extra nutrients.

*Other Potato Toppers*_____

* Turkey bacon and low-fat cheese.
* Mushrooms and low-fat cheese.
* Veggies and low-fat cheese.
* Low-fat cottage cheese and salsa.

🐛 Fruit Salad

Fruit salad is a good balance to this very filling lunch. Chill beforehand, if desired. Use fresh fruits when in season for best taste.

🍎 Turkey Dinner

Preparation Time: About 5 minutes
Cooking Time: 6 to 8 hours, unattended

1 (3-pound) fresh turkey breast
1/4 cup chopped dried onion
2 Tablespoons chopped dried parsley
dash of garlic powder
dash of pepper
dash of paprika

1. Wash turkey breast. Remove all visible skin with kitchen scissors. Rinse under cold water.
2. Place turkey breast in crock-pot. Season with onion, parsley, garlic, pepper, and paprika in crock-pot.
3. Cook on low heat. Let turkey rest 20 minutes before slicing while keeping juices warm in crock-pot.

Yield: *8 servings (4 ounces per serving)*
1 serving contains: 120 Calories   1 g. Fat   55 mg. Sodium

Turkey Tidbit _____

* A boneless, skinless turkey breast tenderloin may be substituted for turkey breast.

🐛 Sweet Potato Casserole

Preparation Time: About 5 minutes
Cooking Time: 30 minutes

2 cans (15-ounce) sweet potatoes, drained
1 can (8-ounce) crushed pineapple
1/4 teaspoon cinnamon
1/4 teaspoon nutmeg
1 cup miniature marshmallows

1. Preheat oven to 350 degrees. In an 8-inch square glass casserole, mash potatoes. Add pineapple, cinnamon, and nutmeg to potatoes. Mix well.
2. Top with marshmallows. Bake until marshmallows are melted and golden brown.

Yield: *8 servings (1/3 cup per serving)*
1 serving contains: 130 Calories   1 g. Fat   10 mg. Sodium

*Sweet Potato Casserole Notes*_____ 🐛

* May be made in advance. Cover and refrigerate until ready to bake.

* Sweet potato mixture may be placed in scooped orange halves and baked as directed for a lovely side dish.

* May prefer to use 2 pounds fresh sweet potatoes that have been baked and skin removed.

❦ Parmesan Squash

Preparation Time: About 5 minutes
Cooking Time: 10 minutes

1 (1/2 pound) zucchini, thinly sliced
1 (1/2 pound) yellow squash, thinly sliced
2 Tablespoons fat-free grated Parmesan cheese
fresh lemon juice, to taste
pepper, to taste

1. Steam vegetables.
2. Top with Parmesan, lemon juice, and pepper.

Yield: *8 servings (1/4 cup per serving)*
1 serving contains: 40 Calories   0 g. Fat   60 mg. Sodium

❦ Cranberry Sauce

Adding cranberries to this dinner is a good blend of flavors and a nice finishing touch to the meal. Chill in refrigerator before serving, if desired.

Personal Notes _____ ❦

_____

_____

_____

_____

_____

Nutritional Info
Day 1 _____

Meal	Serving Size	Calories	Fat grams	Sodium mg.
Breakfast				
Waffle	1 (4-inch)	120	0	225
Strawberries	1/2 cup	50	0	0
Syrup	1/4 cup	100	0	180
Milk	1 cup	80	0	110
Total		**350**	**0**	**515**
Lunch				
Quesadilla	1	170	6.5	310
Veggie Chili	1 cup	150	1.5	445
Pineapple	2 slices	35	0	15
Total		**355**	**8**	**770**
Dinner				
Roast Beef	3 oz.	155	4	200
Potatoes	2/3 cup	100	0	75
Green Beans	1/2 cup	20	0	0
Applesauce	1/2 cup	50	0	0
Total		**325**	**4**	**275**

==

Day 1		*Calories*	*Fat grams*	*Sodium mg.*
Total		*1030*	*12*	*1560*

Nutritional Info
Day 2

Meal	Serving Size	Calories	Fat grams	Sodium mg.
Breakfast				
French Toast	2 slices	120	0	350
Turkey Bacon	2 slices	40	1	130
Apple Slices	1/4 apple	30	0	0
Milk	1 cup	80	0	110
Total		270	1	590
Lunch				
Barbecue Beef	3 oz	335	6	640
Lettuce Salad	1 1/2 cup	50	0	290
and Dressing	1 Tbs	50	0	290
Pear	1 medium	80	0	0
Total		465	6	930
Dinner				
Spaghetti Sauce	1/2 cup	75	0.5	150
Spaghetti Noodles	1 cup	200	1	0
Caesar Salad	1 1/2 cup	45	0	100
Garlic Bread	1 slice	80	0	65
Total		400	1.5	315

===

Day 2	Calories	Fat grams	Sodium mg.
Total	1135	8.5	1835

Nutritional Info
Day 3

Meal	Serving Size	Calories	Fat grams	Sodium mg.
Breakfast				
Yogurt Shake	12 oz.	175	0	70
Granola Crunch	1/2 cup	200	4	195
Total		**375**	**4**	**265**
Lunch				
Macaroni & Cheese	1 cup	270	8	310
Mixed Veggies	2/3 cup	40	0	50
Apple	1 medium	80	0	0
Total		**390**	**8**	**380**
Dinner				
Chicken Breast	4 oz	225	2	370
Wild Rice	1 cup	160	0.5	100
Broccoli	1/2 cup	250	0	10
Fruited Salad	1 1/2 cup	60	1	20
Total		**470**	**3.5**	**500**

===

Day 3	Calories	Fat grams	Sodium mg.
Total	**1235**	**15.5**	**1145**

Nutritional Info
Day 4 _____ ❦

Meal	Serving Size	Calories	Fat grams	Sodium mg.
Breakfast				
Egg Bacon Muffin	1	220	4	425
Apple Juice	6 oz.	84	0	0
Total		**304**	**4**	**425**
Lunch				
Chicken Salad	2 oz chicken			
with Dressing	2 Tbs	225	3	485
Orange Slices	1 orange	65	0	0
Total		**290**	**3**	**485**
Dinner				
Pep Pizza	1/8 pizza	185	6	385
L'Italian Salad	1 1/2 cup			
with Dressing	2 Tbs	40	1	15
Total		**225**	**7**	**405**

==

Day 4		Calories	Fat grams	Sodium mg.
Total		*819*	*14*	*1315*

Nutritional Info
Day 5 _____

Meal	Serving Size	Calories	Fat grams	Sodium mg.
Breakfast				
Oatmeal	2/3 cup	110	1	30
Banana	1 banana	80	0	0
Total		**190**	**1**	**30**
Lunch				
Turkey Club	1	280	4	295
Carrot Sticks	2 carrots	40	0	0
Total		**320**	**4**	**295**
Dinner				
Meatloaf	4 oz.	165	9	75
Bean Casserole	1/2 cup	105	1	260
Baked Potato	1	80	0	0
Fruit Salad	1/2 cup	60	0	5
Total		**410**	**10**	**340**

==

Day 5	Calories	Fat grams	Sodium mg.
Total	920	15	635

Nutritional Info
Day 6_____ 🦐

Meal	Serving Size	Calories	Fat grams	Sodium mg.
Breakfast				
Fruited Nonfat				
Yogurt	1 cup	100	0	140
Blueberry Muffin	1	225	1	50
		-------	-------	-------
Total		**325**	**1**	**190**
Lunch				
Tuna	2 oz			
Sandwich	2 slices	210	5	495
Low-fat chips	12 chips	110	1.5	150
Peach	1 small	80	0	0
		-------	-------	-------
Total		**400**	**6.5**	**645**
Dinner				
Turkey Burger				
and Bun	4 oz	150	3	300
Oven Fries	1 cup	100	0	0
Chinese Slaw	1/2 cup	105	5	160
		-------	-------	-------
Total		**355**	**8**	**460**

===

Day 6	Calories	Fat grams	Sodium mg.
Total	1080	15.5	1295

Nutritional Info
Day 7

Meal	Serving Size	Calories	Fat grams	Sodium mg.
Breakfast				
Pancake	2 cakes	80	0	150
Sausage	2 patties	90	2	150
Syrup	1/4 cup	100	0	180
Blueberries	1/2 cup	50	0	0
Milk	1 cup	80	0	110
Total		**400**	**2**	**590**
Lunch				
Stuffed potato	1 potato			
with veg chili	1/2 cup			
and cheese	1 Tbs	177	1	300
Fruit Salad	1/2 cup	60	0	0
Total		**237**	**1**	**300**
Dinner				
Turkey Breast	4 oz	120	1	55
Swt Potato Cass	1/3 cup	130	1	10
Parm Squash	1/2 cup	40	0	60
Cranberry Sauce	1/4 cup	110	0	35
Total		**400**	**2**	**160**

Day 7	Calories	Fat grams	Sodium mg.
Total	**1037**	**5**	**1050**

Grocery List

To make complete week's menu

Bread & Grains
___ ___ English Muffins
___ ___ Flour Tortillas
___ ___ Oats, Quick Cooking
___ ___ Hamburger Buns
___ ___ Pizza Shell-12 inch
___ ___ Sourdough Bread

Canned Fruits & Juices
___ ___ Apple Juice
___ ___ Applesauce
___ ___ Cranberry Sauce
___ ___ Crushed Pineapple-8 oz
___ ___ Mixed Fruit, No Sugar
___ ___ Orange Juice
___ ___ Pineapple Chunks-8 oz
___ ___ Pineapple Slices

Canned Vegetables & Sauces
___ ___ Barbecue Sauce
___ ___ 2 Beans, French Green
　　　　No Salt-14 1/2 oz each
___ ___ Beans, Garbanzo -15 oz
___ ___ Beans, Kidney,
　　　　Dark Red-16 oz.
___ ___ Chili Sauce
___ ___ Onions, French Small
___ ___ Paste, Tomato-6 oz
___ ___ Sauce, Pepperoni Pizza
___ ___ Sauce, Tabasco
___ ___ Sauce, Worcestershire
___ ___ 2 Sweet Potatoes-15 oz
___ ___ Tomatoes, Low-Sodium-
　　　　14 oz
___ ___ Water Chestnuts-8 oz

Dairy
___ ___ Butter Substitute
___ ___ Cheese, Fat-free
　　　　Parmesan
___ ___ Cheese, Finely Grated
___ ___ Cheese, Processed-
　　　　3/4 oz slices
___ ___ Egg Substitute-
　　　　5 1/2 cups
___ ___ Skim Milk
___ ___ Yogurt, Fruited Nonfat
___ ___ Yogurt, Plain Nonfat
___ ___ Yogurt, Vanilla Nonfat

Fresh Fruit Produce
___ ___ Apples
___ ___ Banana
___ ___ Blueberries, In Season
___ ___ Grapes
___ ___ Lemons
___ ___ Oranges
___ ___ Peaches
___ ___ Strawberries, In Season

Fresh Vegetables Produce
___ ___ Broccoli-2 lb
___ ___ Cabbage Slaw-1 lb
___ ___ Carrots
___ ___ Celery
___ ___ Garlic Cloves
___ ___ Beans, Green -1 lb
___ ___ Lettuce of Your Choice
___ ___ Mushrooms-1 lb
___ ___ 4 Onions
___ ___ Onions, Green
___ ___ Peppers, Green or Red
___ ___ Potatoes, Sweet
___ ___ Potatoes, White
___ ___ Tomatoes
___ ___ Yellow Squash
___ ___ Zucchini

Frozen Foods

___ ___ Blueberries
___ ___ Green Beans
___ ___ Mixed Vegetables
___ ___ Strawberries

Herbs, Spices & Extracts

___ ___ Allspice
___ ___ Apple Pie Spice
___ ___ Basil
___ ___ Bay Leaf
___ ___ Black Pepper
___ ___ Cajun Seasoning
___ ___ Cayenne
___ ___ Chili Powder
___ ___ Cinnamon
___ ___ Creole Seasonings
___ ___ Cumin
___ ___ Curry
___ ___ Dried Chopped Onion
___ ___ Dry Mustard
___ ___ Garlic Powder
___ ___ Ground Cloves
___ ___ Nutmeg
___ ___ Old Bay Seasonings
___ ___ Onion Powder
___ ___ Oregano
___ ___ Paprika
___ ___ Parsley Flakes
___ ___ Salt Substitute
___ ___ Thyme
___ ___ Vanilla Extract

Meat, Poultry & Fish

___ ___ Bacon, Canadian or Turkey
___ ___ Beef, Extra Lean Ground Round-1 lb
___ ___ Beef, Eye of Round- 2 lb
___ ___ Chicken Breasts, Boneless Skinless-6
___ ___ Tuna Fish Packed in Spring Water-6 oz
___ ___ Turkey Breast, Fresh 3 lb
___ ___ Turkey Breast, Ground White Meat-2 lbs

Miscellaneous

___ ___ Almonds, Chopped
___ ___ Anchovy Paste
___ ___ Apricots, Dried
___ ___ Coconut, Unsweetened Shredded
___ ___ Mustard, Course-Grained
___ ___ Mustard, Honey
___ ___ Pecans, Chopped
___ ___ Potato Chips, Low-fat
___ ___ Prunes, Chopped Pitted
___ ___ Raisins
___ ___ Raspberry Preserves
___ ___ Salad Dressing, Fat-free
___ ___ Sunflower Seeds
___ ___ Soup, Beef Ramen, Low-fat
___ ___ Soup, Tomato, Low-fat, Low-sodium-10 3/4 oz
___ ___ Syrup, Lite

Pasta, Rice & Beans

___ ___ Rice, Long Grain & Wild
___ ___ Spaghetti Noodles-16 oz

Staples

___ ___ Baking Powder
___ ___ Baking Soda
___ ___ Bouillon, Instant
___ ___ Bread Crumbs, Italian
___ ___ Broth, Chicken-32 oz
___ ___ Brown Sugar or Substitute
___ ___ Cereal, Wheat Flake
___ ___ Cooking Spray, Nonfat
___ ___ Cornstarch
___ ___ Flour. All- Purpose
___ ___ Mayonnaise, Low-fat
___ ___ Milk, Nonfat Evaporated Skim
___ ___ Oil, Canola
___ ___ Oil, Olive
___ ___ Sugar or Substitute
___ ___ Vinegar, Red Wine
___ ___ Vinegar, Rice Wine

How to Order

To receive additional copies of this cookbook (or inquire about future publications) by returning an order form and your check or money order to:

Betsy Rudolph
P.O. Box 280
Jerseyville IL 62052

✂ --

Please send me _____ copies of *Betsy's* **Blue Plate Specials** at $15.95 per copy. I am enclosing $2.50 for shipping and handling per book. (Illinois residents add $1.15 sales tax per book.)

Mail Books To:

Name_____

Address_____

City_____ State_____ ZIP_____

Make checks payable to Betsy's Blue Plate Specials.